MOTHER

MOTHER

DOROTHEA LASKY

WAVE BOOKS SEATTLE & NEW YORK

Published by Wave Books
www.wavepoetry.com

Wave Books titles are distributed to the trade by
Consortium Book Sales and Distribution
ipage.ingramcontent.com / (800) 937-8200 / ips@ingramcontent.com
Library of Congress Cataloging-in-Publication Data
Names: Lasky, Dorothea, 1978– author
Title: Mother / Dorothea Lasky.
Other titles: Mother (Compilation)
Description: First edition. | Seattle : Wave Books, 2026. |
Identifiers: LCCN 2026009835 | ISBN 9798891060470 paperback
Subjects: LCGFT: Poetry
Classification: LCC PS3612.A858 M68 2026
LC record available at https://lccn.loc.gov/2026009835
Designed by Crisis
Printed in Canada
9 8 7 6 5 4 3 2 1
First Edition
Wave Books 129

For Carole, Hera, Chance, and Violet

The day is different and each day slows it down.

BERNADETTE MAYER

MOTHER

MOTHER

The bird was blue and grey
Lying on the stairs
There was something
Moving inside of it
And still I knew it was dead
I promised my mother
I wouldn't touch anything
That had been long gone
Inside something turned and wiggled
There's a kind of transformation
That can happen on any day
You'd rather cut your head off
Before you see it
You'd rather ignore
The holy body writhing
Knowing that inside of it
It's calling out your name
"Mother"
"Mother"
It's calling out to you
"Mother!"
But will you save it
Just like the others

MOTHER

What does it mean to mourn
The fact that nothing escapes time
I am writing to you 10 weeks pregnant
God willing in 10 weeks
I will be 20 weeks pregnant
But no matter what
That time will pass
I will still somehow be me
But altered
I won't be the same
As that little girl
Who dreamed
About writing these poems to you
I will barely remember
What she thought it would be like
Was it necessity
That forced her to find the words
Year after year
The trees keep changing
And I keep losing friends
I'll wear an orange suit on the day I die
To match the inner sanctum
Of my vicious automobile
Nothing will stop the blessing
Of my son being 16 in a few short years
He promised me he will always be my baby
But I know already from living this long
Time is a promise we're bound to break

MOTHER

When you say Mother
I do not think of the soft bedsheets
Of a grand nurturing
With the music of flowers
Spilling everywhere into the day
I do not think of the nice words of a person
Who loves you better than anyone
Or the gentle eyes of a grand maternal deer
Who is bent over the grasses
Gathered for ten hundred years
Just to take it in the maw
And smash it so gracefully
I do not think of birds
Who carry worms
Over forest and fire
Or who become the large bunny
Made of clouds that hang over
The springish sky
I don't think of any of these things
But perhaps I should
Perhaps I should now
Instead I think of a gun
Pointed always
At my head
I think of lack of breath
As you are running
Far far away from the house
Because someone has told you

To leave
I think of the quiet anger
That never goes away
Perhaps when you say Mother
I should think of every force in the world
That's good
But my thoughts are not that simple
I think of thunder and rain and the
Things that grow after
But when I hear that thunder
I only think of the doom
Of the approaching storm
One that has taken my whole life
To get away from

LOVE IS RED

A spell
A very hard spell is love
It is monstrous because it has no red in it
It is so monstrous ordinarily
Is that any argument for the use of it
Is there not anything that has so much stretched out

A very hard spell is love
Is there not anything as monstrous
As the ordinary red that is so stretched out
A red hat worn so ordinarily
Is that any argument for the use of it
Is there not anything that has so much stretched out

A monstrous red is so stretched out ordinarily
Is there not anything that has a use of it
A spell is very hard on love
Yes a very hard spell is monstrous ordinarily
Is there no argument left for the use of it
Is there not anything left to stretch it out

I PLAYED GOD

I played God
And chose someone I didn't even know
Every woman plays God
And chooses something they don't even know
And makes their selection
Among a faulty grouping
Every woman plays God
And makes their money
Among people
She doesn't even know
Making a choice
With people
She doesn't even know
We all play God
When the bomb drops
From our hand
Just like a ball
Happy New Year's Eve
Every woman plays God
When she drops the ball
From a hand
She doesn't even know
But it's her hand
Every woman celebrates
The night
God created everything
Every woman takes a hand
That doesn't belong to her
And says: that one

PROGESTERONE LOVE POEM

Calm killer
Infused in the needle
I hold it up to the light
To alight my senses
I remember when I was young
And you came in multitudes
Now my dreams are rough
I slither on the wooden ground
Everything is a reason to dread
Push yourself into me
If they make you love me
Maybe I can be immortal again

MOTHER

I am not the same as another mother
Who took away all of the food
From her daughter
From the moment she could swallow
Eventually leaving her to die
With grey lips in a sallow room
Or the mother who in tan and stripes
Humbles along with her children
At the first bell of school
Everything all ready
As always, never not ready to be
I am not the mother who sleeps
Through dance classes
Or the one who drinks cocktails
I am not the mother all in vegetables
Or tonics, wearing clogs on the way
Or the mother who longs
For some sense of youth
And will do anything to get it back
Or the ceramic cat
That no one will allow themselves
To get away from
I do not take vacations
To places with the sun and sand
No instead I stay inside
I stay in here each day boiling eggs
And putting apple juice
Into tiny cups and screaming

At nearly everyone who is around
I am not the kind of mother
Who waits patiently for the bell
I am the mother who does not
Listen to the bell at all
And all of the toxic femininity
Of every lesson
No I do not learn it
I am not the mother who complains
About changing
I am the mother who begrudgingly
Always changes
In fact I'll change now
I'll be the demonic mother
Who reminds you all not to forget
Exactly who you are
And when they come for you
When they come for your throat
And steal the best parts of you
I am the mother who will fight them
I am the mother who won't give up
Until I've fought them to the ground

MOTHER

Mother I went in the rose garden
In the middle of the night
To find the things I lost there
Mother I searched for you
For seven nights
And could not find you
They left your perfume everywhere
A kind of toying aspect
And scratched your picture
With their talons
I replaced it
Despite their anger
And still got up in the morning
To feed the babies
Their first meal
Mother I wore a lilac dress
And stepped through the thistle
The alligators had already overtaken
The endless landscape
Your body was somewhere there
And it was my job to bury it
But I couldn't
In my head your voice rang out
With the strangest aroma
The gods had left you in the rose garden
Mother I went in before dawn to find you
I didn't know they left
So many noxious animals

There to hurt me
Terrible fear upon terrible fear
Mother I was motherless
So I became myself finally
I wandered in the endless garden
To find something I had lost
When I finally gave up
Mother the roses they overtook me
I filled with vines and lead
And waited two hundred years
Mother I waited there forever
Searching and searching
Until they let you in again

RADICAL MOTHERHOOD

I sat drowsy in a chair waiting for the news
She came back to tell me
That I was fixed
Weeks before I had waited in the same chair
To hear I had 17 eggs
I did not know yet what you would be
Six years earlier your sister
I pushed her out so quickly
I think I was thinking of something else
I just wanted to get through it
I knew it would be ok
All I wanted was an egg sandwich
My doctor in a pink sweater
Said with the next one it would be better
That gave me an idea
On which I placed a whole heap of hope
Your brother came next
I loved him so much I wanted you
I fought a good fight for you
Your father, who had ideas of his own
My body which was scarred and old
And too fat, which they all told me about
I ate eggs and no carbs for months
No chocolate, no juices
I took so many shots
Only some of them hurt
We were all inside because of the virus
Your dad got sick first

But that part was fine
That was months earlier
When I couldn't stop coughing
Or smell the patchouli
For years I wanted you
I was willing to do anything
And believe me I did
There was just nothing else I wouldn't have done
That's how much I loved your brother
To know that you'd be similar
My beautiful little baby
Someday, as they say, you'll understand

MOTHER AND CHILD

When you were born they took you from me
Now they're going to take you from me again
Sticking a tube down your throat
While they assure me it's fine
And to get back to work
After all there's an economy to save

Years later I imagined a more normal setting
Of you in a blanket and me not so crass
The country instead lined up the tiny coffins
They knew the earth was gone by now
Even more vehemently they prayed to the god of money
They said shove off as they kicked me into a ditch

BAD TEACHER

I'm wild
But I'm not evil
I'm not the evil teacher
Who sits at the front of the classroom
I sit in the back of the classroom
With the bad boys
It's all so lovely and awful
This way of life
And I can shout
With the best of them
Anyway something is wrong
With Mommy
Her head is just completely off now
She's wild
And entirely evil
She sits in the front of the classroom
And from her severed head
She smiles at me
And even when I close my eyes
I can see she's still smiling at me
Anyway something is wrong with me
I can sit in the back of the classroom
And see my severed head
Somewhere floating
It looks so angry
And even when I close my eyes
I can tell it's still angry at me

THE C-SECTION

The night before it happened
I knew what would be the outcome
I saw myself fleshy and full of Betadine

The inevitable
Halved and quartered
Then alone in the stark white room

Should I have been surprised
No no, no who would be
Life is money, then dick

Then breathing
Live for the moment
When you're whole, you can't see

Anyway, wholeness?
Why do it
Wholeness: Don't be

MOTHER

Mothering
It's not evil to me
The women are what it is—
The rulers of nature

Someday all of the world will blow up in a curse
And so be it—
The difference between that and a cure
Is a tiny snake

And when she says, I am she,
You think it's the devil
But no, it's a victory—
Yes I would cross the river of rats for you

The book at the end
Which had turned in on itself—
Which had always been open
To the page about desire

Be true to yourself
Choose another mother—
Today is an eyeball
It sits in the head, forgetting itself

Losing your mind to love but you don't own it
When it is found
It never was there—
Lonely miniatures, always about control

The problem with everything—
Is that most people stand speechless
For too long in front of each other
And don't relate: they've always been together

I remember you as young
Your wooden voice—
I'm here, I'm here
You said

A hole that goes on forever
Not the one you caused
But the loss of you—
The hardest lesson is that I came from that

And if you're asking
No one loves anyone more than the dead
Anger as the brightest color—
Yes I would cross the river of rats for you

WAITING

This is very powerful indeed
This is the difference between it all
Now as I hurtle toward heaven
I get an understanding of the muscular sense
What you meant by angels
When I crowned the demons for everything
What you meant I couldn't have believed
So green we were
Now I shatter at each movement
Six days six nights I sat and thought
Of nothing except the pink smoke
Emanating from my abdomen
It was dark inside my room
And outside a storm screaming
I never felt closer to you
Although you were 10000 miles away at least
Or how far are we from the dead
If I knew that though
I wouldn't be who I am
I wouldn't be who I am
Which is living
Which is totally alive
Which is what frightens you
Because somehow you're already dead
And I'll always be living
And when you die
And I die
I'll still be alive

And you'll be dead
So dead
You were born dead
And I was born alive
And I'll die alive
And in between I will be living
And you will never get away from me
That which begs to nag
Because you were born dead
And I died alive
And the plants and things
They know that I'm their mother

FOOD FOR BABIES

Oranges and hot chocolate
And mittens
Cookie milk
Eggs both scrambled and over easy
English muffins with butter
And fruit tape
Apple juice by the gallon
Bacon and grilled cheese
Pizza and brussels sprouts
String beans and rotisserie chicken
Fish, or more specifically, salmon
And candy bags that were hidden
With chocolate coins
And watermelon lollipops
Spinach and tomato puffs
Puffs seeped in broth
Steak and hamburgers
Cheeseburgers with ketchup
Cheeseburgers without ketchup
Burgers without ketchup
French fries
French fries without ketchup
Apples and cheese
Egg rolls and spring rolls
Orange juice and water
Water from the Berkey
And water from the tap
Cucumbers without the peel

Salted on English muffins
Applesauce
Ice cream cake on birthdays
It's so sweet
Now I'll have a nightmare
Sweet green cake
I baked it for you on your birthday
Clean up your toys
I fucking asked you to do it
The oranges are too sweet
They are too sour
The clementines are rotten
The clementines have a thick film of mold
Growing from their skin
Strawberries that only last a day
Even in the refrigerator
Going to sleep too late
I stuffed my face
I am throwing up now
I am throwing up into the tub
Get me a show
I had an accident
I had an accident in my bed
I am tired tuck me in
It's cold in here
The water is cold
The water is too hot
Turn down the water
I won't get in that cold water
Where are the cookies
I will eat the gummy bunnies

Where is my dinner
Give me my French fries
If you don't eat your dinner
You can't have dessert
If you don't clean up your toys
You can't have dessert
I fucking asked you to do it
School is in ten minutes
If you get too many lates
You will have to repeat again
If you don't finish this homework
Your teachers will be angry
Do you want to make
Your teachers angry
Oranges and hot chocolate
The oranges are rotten
Grilled cheese on sourdough toast
With lots of butter
I see you like ketchup on eggs
I said for you to do it
I am crying
Why aren't you in here
I am scared you will die
I am so sorry I yelled
I am just so tired
I fucking told you to do it
I am tired
So tired
Even I can't comprehend how
Tired I am
Orange juice on toast

Cookie milk on butter
Pizza is in the oven
I mashed the fish into the brussels sprouts
The green beans are too spicy
I don't like these noodles
Take the green things off the noodles
The green things!
Will you die
When you go to the hospital
I fucking told you to do it
I fucking told you to do it
Do it
Do it
Do it
I dare you

PERIOD AT 43

Maybe it was always violence
It took the girl for me to see
That the blood smeared everywhere
Wasn't really ok
That it made me special
But also cursed with powers
And that everyone would fear me for it

For so many years
I learned to avoid white shorts
Now I long for it
Like the way you long for a lover
Who you don't even know too well
In some ways that's the best kind
Seeing them in a shocking way
In the hazy hall light of mistaken identity

Now I keep the whitest pads
Close to me always
I want to know just exactly
How none will come out
Because seeing it in these months
Would be the worst crime
Would mean I failed again
Would mean they were always right about me

ROSEMARY

I wrote in my diary about a demon
Which everyone assumed was me
Who could blame them
When it was me who birthed it
When my long nails took it off inside of me
What they never realized is the doubling effect
Of when you hurt yourself
And can hurt them, too
Still they laid me out
And had their way with me
I kept insisting that the diary
Held all of the answers
Looking so forlorn and excitable
Pale and hungry for raw eggs and sugar
They wanted me just to sit there
And have it all done to me
But I got out of that pale blue dress
I took myself to the cemetery
I said, please please, Mother, I'm starving
Won't you open that big heavy latch
Won't you let me in

POEM FOR MY DAUGHTER

You've come to so many conclusions
But this will be the lasting one
A green egg holding the space of an idea
That is wholly yours

Keep asking questions, you will get answers
The right answers, the wrong answers, but answers
You will live on and see the deer bending so gently to drink
What's better than any of this you will ask others

To yourself, you will ask nothing
You will only dream, and dream well
And write down your dreams in a silver notebook
Only to be washed away one day by rain

Dream sweetly, my little daughter
Someday you will hate me
Until then let's pretend
That all we have are dreams and wishes

PAIN

Hunger as a man in the darkness peeking out
Stripped down to some kind of essence
I am crazy but I am also fabulous
I said barely walking
I crunched over my back
So that I couldn't hurt my abdomen
The birds scared me
When I was all alone in the half-dark
Orange and blue birds
And I was hot all over
They kept calling to say
It was the worst day ever
And then they didn't call at all
I sat at the round table
Ready for anything
The kind of lilacs you gather
Because you have to
I said everything I could
And it was still vapid and ugly
She said it was the worst holiday
She had ever experienced
Every moment I hurt
Every moment I wished just for stasis
A firm heartbeat
The sound of rustling inside of me
A blue vein or two
Popping from my thigh
I paid her everything

Just to quiet down my abdomen
Everyone said it had been the worst night ever
But for me it was just one long night
While they slept
I paid my debts with
Everything stolen from me
The flies flew into my nostrils
It was the kind of red night
You gather when that's all you can do
I said this is the worst moment ever
And then it was over
And then it was all I could do

SEXUAL

So sexually repressed
But they aren't mothers

The bed is bleeding
But will you sleep in it

What is time
In the space of the infinite

Almost everything timed is a trigger
A trigger to my unhappiness

Everyone evil is alone
I'm alone so I must be evil, too

Hot sex and gold
But I'm alone

Hot sex and gold
I must be evil, too

BIRTH

When I was born I didn't cry
Instead they pulled me out a giant lifeless doll
And sat me on the glass table
All of the doctors ran
Eventually it was fine
When Hera was born
She looked like a clear bubble
Encasing a red lamb
I barely got to see her
As they raced her out of the room
When my son was born
They pulled him out of me
The doctor came over
Hours later, my gristle all over
Her smock and said
It all turned out ok
I couldn't move anything
Under my eyelids
Birth is everything they said it would be
And the death doulas also make
Their proclamations into the afternoon
Yes you see narcissism or the self
Is the gift of the mother
You might say that this is disgusting
And you'd be right
But so is everything
So are you
So is life

So look deep into the mirror now
My beloved
Aren't you the happy genius
Of your little household
Without art we'd all just be
Swimming upstream with the tax collector
So look deep into that slick surface
So much had to die to put you there
It's not wrong to respect yourself
That person that you'll always be

MOTHER

Once alone I couldn't help
But remember how much I am hated
And then the similar feelings
About why am I here
I hadn't felt this way
In so many months
But now I was scared again
My own mother used to
Make a big performance of it
And lock me out of her bedroom
It must have felt so glamorous
To hear your child
Call and call
Now when I say I want to die
Everyone turns around
And keeps doing what they were doing
But who can blame them
Mental illness is a burden
I know that better than anyone
I'll never leave this house again
I'll just sit here consumed
By dreams that are long sour
Maybe the orange that is everywhere
Is really taunting me for no reason
I am tired so tired
I can't even express how tired I am

EVERYONE HATES PREGNANT WOMEN

People are so scary
Like boats docked
In the middle of the ocean
Like sand gulls
Bleating
When it's never dinnertime
Language flows
But they hate me
And I don't feel like any of this
Motherhood, getting up
All of the screams and shots
It's all over for me, Charlie Brown
No one likes a woman anyway
It's all just perfectly adequate
Bursting and it's medicated
Little jewel
Safe in the box that the mice can't get to
Perfectly placed in the center of three chairs
The cow jumping over the green moon
Where the bedroom is safe and innocent
Like a real heart
That you can hold in your hands
Its skin feels soft like a rose petal
Or a cat tongue
It's giving me so much love
In the magic number square
All of the dreams of my semi-youth
Now completely lost

In knee-deep water
It's not water though it's blood
And it might be mine or yours
Whatever the case it's my job to make it
And to clean it up
Everyone says, do it do it
While they sit there
And I'm sweating and contorting
In a mirrored room
Where I can't even see myself
But you know one day soon
I'll wear a pretty dress again
And saunter into the golden ballroom
A spicy someone will meet me there
Or no he will actually be quite calm
He will take my hand just like the others
But in his eyes I will know it was all worth it
And when I say I love you how are you
He will say oh thanks for asking
But no this isn't the way it will end
I will go gliding through
With everyone watching
And it will be inevitable how I win again
I've got so much before me
And even as the poems run away from me
In less than an hour
I know they will come back
No one owns poetry
It only goes through you
As soon as you realize that you will be actually happy
It's all a source of comfort

You see poetry was always there when no one else was
You see poetry was my friend when I was tiny
Alone in the dirt
Looking for somewhere to put these yellowed roots
And grow
And even though I've totally bashed it
On every day of my cursed life
It was still always my funny little eagle
Coming back again and again
To eat from my stubby fingers
And lack of wrists
And big and meaty arms connected to a sack
Of loose skin
And even though I told everyone
I didn't need it
It knew I did
And forgave me anyway
Because it's not about poetry being bad or good
It's about poetry living or dying
And poisoning everyone

THREE DAYS

I ate an orange
In the blue pregnancy chair
While they watched a show
About modern vampires
And I thought about whenever
My period does come back
It will be light just like before
And only last a few days at most
And then eventually
It will taper off entirely
For 33 years it has been
A marker of time
A light of hope
When everything around me
Couldn't be trusted
I could trust that blood wash
To flood everywhere
And even though I've spent
Eight months now
Dreading the sight
Of anything red
Now I long to bleed all over
The chair
And make a mess
Just like the poem
About a sexual act
That looks like a murder scene
I want to make a scene once again
Now all of that bleeding

Will fold into my voice like an echo
But it's not the saddest thing
The saddest thing would be to die
With a ventilator on my face
Knowing there was nothing left
No the saddest thing
Would be to be killed
When I was young
Bleeding from every wound
In the dream he bumped the baby
And I screamed
But no one could help me
I wake every moment
In a frenzy of what could happen
What doesn't happen is bleeding
I have stopped it up
With a false hormonal cork
What doesn't happen is the egg
Instead it's now a human growing
What may never happen is that
I'll fold over just like the dance
And wear the gold queen dress
And everyone will say
Wow that's amazing
No instead the book is bad
It's always been a bad book
And I'll throw this stick at you
Because somehow I've done something
So wrong just by being here
And one of the few things
I thought I could count on
Is leaving me

WATER HOLDS NO NEW MEMORIES

When your mother leaves
You will call for her
And wish almost
More than anything
That she were still here

But of course when she was
You cursed her
And wished almost more than anything
That you could have a life
Entirely without her

Orange cream, and black cream
And cream spilling everywhere
It's all thick and soupy
Like soap stuck to the bottom
Of the bathtub

That dumb layer
All of those happy moments
You rinsed off
While thinking about
Something else entirely

Will you wish for them back
Red cream, and yellow cream
If you had to do it over again
Say it!
You wouldn't

C-SECTION

What day is your C-section
Shouldn't they be scheduling
The C-section by now
I had a natural birth
I didn't have a C-section
I had three C-sections
You know you're having
A C-section
So why not schedule it
So we know when to
Schedule our doctors' appointments
We will get the car
Depending on the day
And time of your C-section
C-sections are so easy
You don't need to do
Anything
There's the medical theatre
We know you are very performative
So won't you like it
C-sections are totally routine
So many women have them
C-sections aren't really
Like birthing
They are more like lying back
Could you pull your pants down
Over your stomach
Could you pull your underpants down

This won't hurt at all
No you won't feel a thing
Just some slight tugging
Then we will put
It all back in
What day will you do your C-section
It's easier on us
If you schedule it now
Don't you think it would be nice to know
Tell us the date
What day is your C-section
We'd like to know
So that we can organize
Our doctors' appointments
And other plans
Accordingly

DO IT FROM THE GUT

There's so much to the world that you don't know
Even now as the afternoon is fading
You move one thin film to the next
You could sit here and dream
Instead you'll get up and do the thing
In an hour it will be dark again
It's all a great green mystery
The colorful bird is back
This time he's telling you to be quiet

WORST

I am the worst kind of person
Protecting my little male babies at every turn
Motherhood is ultimately hard on the mother
Green cherries hanging from the trees
It's by misspelling that I learn the real words

Protecting my little male babies at every turn
Green cherries hanging from the trees
It's by misspelling that I learn the real words
I am the worst kind of woman
Motherhood is ultimately hard on the mother

Hard on the mother motherhood is ultimately
Green cherries and the worst kind of woman
I am my little male babies
Only by protecting the words
Only by misspelling do I learn the real words

IT

Neon red devil
I feel safer with you than anyone
Because it's not about the action
It's about the compulsion
Neon red cross
That I took from its wall
And smashed the glass cases
You light up
A dark room
And that's me always
The dark room
Where I go to feel every pain
Because all of this
It absolutely hurts
And the worst part of it is you die
After all of this is over
The worst part of it is you die
And no one remembers who you really were
Oh friends
I died
And none of you knew who I really was

YELLOW AND GREEN

I should say that this is the greatest beginning
Waiting for water until these words are out
But instead I can't think of anything but fear

To know exactly what might happen
Is to be a divine thing, knowing the edges
And I'd never want to be that, even if they promised

That it would give me endless sight
Into the very darkest parts of the day
I'd never want to see those wretched moments anyway

Instead I'll sit here and wait for it
They say the pain is the absolute worst part of waiting
But I say pain is a kind of melody

The worst part are these flowers on the nightstand
They tell me that there's more to live for
But I'm not so sure there's more to live for than this

Sparkle and green will be the day
In the yellow sky a type of delight
A dream of everything is a yellow flower

THE AFTERNOON

I dreamt about suicide for close to 40 years
Auras of spring energy will abound even in the midst of autumn
This poem is not about what dies
But about what lives
Buried in the rubble
Like life is in the semen
Like life is in the womb
This is a poem about dying completely

All my energy they wanted so voraciously
Just to be around it
I couldn't share it anymore
Inside I curled it under the earth
And waited for someone, anyone
I needed so desperately to be cared for

Even the so-called people I had loved
Were too busy to have met the day
I looked only at tall buildings
And ate butter
There's a kind of madness in every joke
And I needed to escape it

There's a kind of living you do
When you might as well do it amorphously
Inside the hotel
Inside the hospital
Inside the unit
I did not leave any of it for months

No one called
No one cared
If I fell I had to pick myself back up
If I cried I had to wipe my own face
If they called for me in the night
I had to be the one to answer the call

It's an utterly tenuous existence
To bend back the layers
And find there was never anything there
I could only look askew while typing
And start breathing into the cup
And start saying things so amorphously

Still I woke up
This poem isn't about suicide
This poem is about life
If you haven't known everybody
Dumb windmills
Then you might as well just survive all of this

It's a wild timing
This existence
It's a brutal calling
This vocation
In the brutal hotel
I entered and existed

What to say about anything
I slept until you stole everything from me
But I had to be the one to get up
And do everything

Everything is always a new memory
The day is on repeat, over and over again

Start again without dying amorphously
This is a poem entirely about suicide
When I felt that way doubled
And when I was empty again
It would call and call
Red leather bed which I called home

Start again while living vicariously
This is a poem not about dying
This is a poem about living
What they take from you
Won't be this
Use it all gracefully
Life is in the semen
Life is in the womb

ROSES

After all of this is over
I'll just be empty again
And it will be the same feelings
Going there and up again
With my arms outstretched
Flat and my palms up
I will lie to receive the rose petals
That the humans have brought for me
I will no longer crave sugar
In the middle of the night
Or palely look for meat
In everything
I will exude dark elixirs
And sweet milks
From every orifice
And will be a source
Like the Willendorf
Foretelling a tale
That mothers will say
Only to their sons
After all of this is over
I will just be empty again
And will long for my stomach
Hanging over everything
I will long for the ascetic twitch
Of never knowing what I will eat
I will no longer crave sugar
I will eat what they tell me to

And do what they tell me to
I will no longer
Crave anything
After all of this is over
I will be powerless again

THE BIRTH

The birth isn't about poetry
It is about screaming pain on a Sunday
Hailing a cab and head racing
The hospital now so close to the new apartment

I had a baby inside of me
But no one expected it to happen so fast
Or at least they said they didn't
Maybe they expected it to happen so fast all along

Alone in the waiting room I shook and shook
The blood ran down my legs
Later with the magnesium
I thought of the many permutations of the bald head

Pale, pickling fish skin, glowing with scales
When she came out, she was dark and full of hair
No blood, but born in the caul
Another magical reality of my past accomplishments

When she came out she cried
It sounded like me
But not me
It was her new reality

Three weeks later, they say I am not an erotic object
So I wander in the snowy park with a friend
We light candles and pray to the darkness
We light the park on fire and they find us

When they take us away
I say: no, this isn't right
I am a mother after all
They say: Mother, but where is your baby

I know now
I do I do
Look, look, look and listen
My beautiful baby, she's here

A BAD DAY

It's a day without sunshine
A year without birthdays
A time without time

It was one day
Stretched into a year
I rose into the night

Still I hope
Everything with you
Is still green and beautiful

I hope you have a very nice
Time at whatever it is
You do there

DON'T LEAVE DOTTIE

Don't leave Dottie
Don't leave child
No matter how they get into your mind
With their poisons
Black cream and orange cream
Red cream everywhere
Yes it's scary
But you're so strong
The dream or the fish
Lost in no water
You will remember
How nothing good comes out of
Knowing any of this
Remember that the poison of their words
Is just that
And that nothing good comes out of giving up
Don't leave child
Don't leave Dottie
It's still your time

DEMON MOTHER

Long live our mothers
Horror and Poetry
Forever
Carole
Natalie
And The Rose
Wendy
And Chaka
Iris
And Tina
Prince
And Florence
Devendra
Lorraine
Sinéad
And Zelda
And the others
Like Dorothea
Demon evil wish
Mother Suspiria
Mother of Whispers
Katie
Lucie
Eileen
And Rebecca
Demon Mother
Demon Mother
Angel Mother

Wake up!
Live!
Live to tell
My Angel Mother
Demon Mother
Live again

TWO MEN AND A CAR CRASH

In the dream they were going to
Listen to the baby's heartbeat
But they had to do it in a car
So I buckled in and they faced me
There were two of them
And I said I was 24 weeks
And proud about it
But also scared as I said it
As they were supposed to measure me
And do the things
While the car was parked in the parking lot
But now we were moving and the car was going
Very fast up onto the highway
And I realize now this was how
Those awful drivers insisted on the highway
On the way to the hospital
And also how the people
Who didn't believe in the pandemic
Made sure to breathe on you
And as the car went faster and faster
I tried to trust the men driving
But I didn't really want to
They weren't even looking at the road
They were looking at me directly
But still I knew it was the polite thing to do
To trust them and they expected me to
And soon the car was driving off the ravine
And as we went into the free space
I didn't think about how I was going to die
I only thought about the baby

LITTLE BABY

Little baby on the edge of the bed
With the room bathed in purple
Didn't you know about the car
That was drenched in magenta light
You were there when it went
Down the road and back again
Little baby on the edge of the bed
You were there with me for that whole fall
When I fell for myself again
Little baby when they took you out
Wasn't it all so obvious
Wasn't it all so exposed like they wanted it
Little baby they had to cut my babies from me
Because I'll never give up on you so easily
Little baby on the edge of the bed
With the room bathed in purple
Wasn't I always a different person
Little baby there on the bed
If I could do it all over again
Little baby there in the room
Drenched in purple
If I could do it all over again
I wouldn't
Little baby
If I could do it all over again
I would

TWO MONTHS

I've never lived any days as a mother without fear
From the first second
Dark green until these light green days
It was never a celebration
It was just people taking my baby from me
Over and over again
They told me two months means
Anything could happen
The novelty of spring
Where everything goes into pastels
Where there might be flowers
But instead it's more pastels
More candies
Now they tell me that things won't be safe
Until two months
But I've lived ten years or more
In fear for the next time
I have never breathed in a sigh
Only one tiny moment of rest after another
Accumulating into something called a life
Even now I hear cries
They are taking her from me again
But they tell me until two months none of it
Means anything
I've never lived any days as a mother
Without this horrible fear
At two months they say it will be better
But after then
What then

NOTHING LIKE THAT FEROCIOUS LOVE

Nothing like that ferocious love
To hold you back in the middle of the night
Only now I am so empty again
It's the same day
But everything has changed
As I go through the middle of the night
In an ice storm
Just praying I can make it here or there
Or back at home
And don't you want to cry
Cause it hurts
But if I lied
If I lied
I'd say none of this
And if I lied
I'd say I loved every second of it
Every damned second of it
All of the pop medicine
And after it happens
Well won't you feel so happy again
Oh, Mother Mother
Mother!
Won't you save her
Just like the others

THE COLORFUL BIRD

You should smile through the pain
And instead of thinking about it
You should think of a colorful bird
With orange and green feathers
He might be a cockatoo
The bird from the poem
Or you may have made him up entirely
Whatever you have to do
There is a board on your wall full of feathers
Someday all of this will be over

THE LAST MOMENTS OF THE EGG

There is a tiny window
Where it still breathes
You can hardly keep anything dry
It's there realizing the heathens
In the most tacky cascade imaginable
People don't think of fluids
As they are meant to be thought of
A word is a thought
Is a masticating liquid
That brings down the essence
Of life itself
You can't hold it back
You can do things to make it happen
But you can't hold it back
In the last day of its vibrance
It will whisper to you in ghosts
I saw one
At the doorway
He said drop everything
I want to be here again
Instead I did something else
For someone else
The egg died
One day that will be me
A clear and everpresent fluid
In someone's lap
One day all I'll be
Is a constantly blooming rose

In someone's lap
Whispering save me save me
Will you
Will you save me

ALL THE COLOR'S DRAINED

There's a pallor
Over every area of my life now
Even the sitting room
Bright and grey
Is drenched of its antiquity
Enervated is what she said
On that final bed
Remembering not if her eyes
Were open or still
But inside the warmth of oceans
From where I came
Now what do I discover
Not the doctor's office yet
But art, life, and the light
Bright white where inside
The blue is everlasting
Until then now everything
Is quite a mood
Every second a new ordinary thing
Made to terrify
Every face you knew since birth
Disfigured to scare you
Until you also leave
There's a funeral
Over every area of my life now
Mother will I also see you
When I cross that river
From where you now go

I hope you will take care
And think of me
I'll think of you
In these days
And also after
Like an entire sandpit of grace
Mother will you remember me
In the spaces where memory
Does not exist
They said I was hers
Now that's a lie
I'm no one's
I can do anything
What now
The water, the light, the dread

IN MY MOTHER'S TOMB

An airplane
An airplane conductor

By the time I was her age
I was already a poet

I was already me
I hope she will never die

And have my fate
To be hated and revered

Red ivy winding
Out of the forest

The golden face
That turns round the corner

It's playing a game
It's having fun with you

They said to be scared
Of the afterlife

And to not see it
So stately and green

But I'm not scared
I live here

I’ve lived here
For as long as I can remember

Mother Mother
I shall decorate your tomb

With pictures of witches
But you were never a witch

I never was anything
Only in knowing so

I became the thing
Forests and soft milk

Let these things be neverending
They shall never take from us

The green scream

MOTHER

Mother, I meant to bring you
The song Sisters of Mercy
But you died before I had time
They found you eating cereal
The angels about you
But no one could see the angels but Daddy
He was holy in his forgetfulness
He even forgot your name
Thirty years in a whirlpool he did not know
What he was about to confess to God upon your death
I liked your heart in this way
No longer suffering
There was a greenness to the air
That we could all live and sleep
Daddy forgetting himself
The floor stained with urine
Yellow moons around every bit of floor
Six dried dirt spots around the tub
That rang only in their plainness
I like earth, that it is plain
I like the softness of sleep, that it floats like air
Upon a dream I once had of a turquoise woman
Who told me to shut my mouth
But she didn't do so in a mean way
She closed my lips
Her fingers full of dew
And in quietude, I heard the hanging of a thousand men
Is it holiness to go away?

I do not know
I'll never go away
I'll live on the earth for a hundred years
And when I leave, it won't even be going
You will hear my voice in a hundred thousand years
The children can hear me whistling for them
They do not think I am graceful
But they think my arms are soft
They think I am warm as they nestle upon me
They call me a great grandmother
I am only the stars that glisten in the black night
I am only the stars that the lovers view
As they begin to know what must be kept upon them
They shuffle each other's hair in front of me
And I am gentle in front of them
I communicate nothing but kindness
Gentle kindness
The kind of kindness we all enjoy

THE LODGE AT MOUNT RAINIER

On the mount, a sunny day
The poems will never be food
The soul of poetry is the mother soul
All the babies who've been cut
All the mothers who've been cut
All the sailors taken from their mothers
All the babies cut from their mothers
This is the thing they fight for:
A blue sky
Silence!
You'll never be food for anyone
Your poems will toil and toil for no reason
All the babies who've been taken
Screaming from their mothers
Out into the lawn
To scream the greenest scream
The silent poems
Are the soul of poetry
Not the baby screaming
Not the person screaming on the hill
On the mount, the most worn down flower
Its frost a fire
In the fire-frost I am its mother
Flower mother don't go
The soul of poetry is on the mountain
The soul of mothers is the poem
That goes on forever, never said
The mother soul is a flower

Flowers say nothing
To the poems that are its food
Mother, poetry is the food of being
The words will never be poems
The poems won't fight they will be quiet
Quiet tiny flowers are stars
The only breath of flowers the poems
That scream into the lawn
The poems are always
Taken from their mothers too soon

ACKNOWLEDGMENTS

Thank you to my friends and family for their support. Thank you to Joshua Beckman and everyone at Wave Books. Thank you to the following journals for originally publishing some of the poems in this book: *American Poetry Review*, *Amsterdam Review*, *Copenhagen*, *The New Yorker*, *Notre Dame Review*, *The Paris Review*, *Poetry*, *The Poetry Foundation blog*, and *The Spectacle*.